The FRAGILE EARTH

John Baines and Barbara James

Illustrated by Maggie Brand

SIMON & SCHUSTER

LONDON • SYDNEY • NEW YORK • TOKYO • TORONTO

Contents

Introduction   5

1. Greenhouse Effect
Global Warming   6
Turning Down the Heat   8

2. The Ozone Layer
A Hole in the Sky   10
Patching the Ozone Hole   12

3. Acid Rain
Poisoning the Environment   14
The Road to Recovery   16

4. Nuclear Energy
A Nuclear Future?   18
Energy Saving   20

5. Radioactive Waste
Waste Not Wanted   22
Not in My Backyard   24

6. Culture Loss
Vanishing Tribes   26
Survival Against the Odds   28

7. Waste and Pollution
Our Polluted World   30
Cut Down, Clean Up   32

8. City Life
Urban Explosion   34
A Better Life?   36

9. Changing Direction
The Price of Progress   38
Politics and the Green Movement   40

Glossary   42
Further Information   43
Index   44

Introduction

People are like all other animals: they need to use what the environment provides to survive. Unlike other animals, humans try to change the environment to improve their lives. For example, to grow more food farmland can be created by clearing woodland or draining swamps. To get from one place to another more quickly a road might be built, and so on. This is called development. The resources that the world provides can run out if we do not use them carefully. Looking after the earth so it continues to provide the resources that all life needs is called conservation.

This book looks at some of the ways in which people damage the environment. It also shows what we can do to try to protect the environment while still enjoying some or all of the benefits of development. This is the challenge of the 1990s. The future of our fragile planet depends on us facing up to this challenge, sooner rather than later.

City pollution: this sign on a busy street in Tokyo, Japan, displays levels of air pollution and noise.

GREENHOUSE EFFECT — 1

Global Warming

In 1988 huge areas of the USA's Mid-West were affected by the worst drought ever. Fields that usually produced thousands of tonnes of maize and other crops produced nothing. Many scientists say that, in the future, such disasters will happen more often as the greenhouse effect makes the earth warmer.

Energy from the sun heats and lights the earth. The atmosphere that surrounds the earth spreads the heat more evenly around the globe, prevents the earth from becoming too hot or cold and causes rain to fall. Together the sun and the atmosphere make life on earth possible.

There are about thirty gases in the upper atmosphere that trap the heat and slow down its escape into space. These so-called greenhouse gases, such as carbon dioxide, methane and water vapour, have existed naturally for millions of years. The amount of some of these gases is increasing, however, and human-made greenhouse gases, such as chlorofluorocarbons (CFCs), are entering the atmosphere as well. The natural balance has been upset and the earth is getting warmer.

The temperature of the earth changes naturally by a few degrees, but over many thousands of years. This has caused ice ages in the past. Over the last 150 years temperatures have increased by between 0.3°C and 0.7°C, most probably as a result of the increase in greenhouse gases. Over the next 40 years, temperatures could rise by another 1.5°C to 4.5°C, a speed of increase never experienced on earth before.

Climate catastrophe

As the temperature increases, the huge polar ice-cap will begin to melt. This could cause sea-levels to rise by about 1.5 metres over the next 60 years. Low-lying areas will be flooded unless expensive sea defences are built. Millions of people are likely to lose their land and their homes. Worst affected would be delta areas, such as Bangladesh, and low-lying oceanic islands. But the consequences of global warming will be felt world-wide.

The world's climate, vegetation and agriculture patterns will change. Weather conditions will become more extreme, with stronger winds, heavier rain and worse droughts. Areas in which food crops are grown could become too hot and dry to support agriculture. Some communities of plants and animals may disappear altogether.

Main picture Greenhouse gases are produced by vehicle exhaust emissions, aerosol sprays, rotting plant and animal matter, and the burning of fossil fuels. As more and more of these gases enter the upper atmosphere, they prevent heat escaping from the earth and the temperature rises. If this process continues, the vast Antarctic ice sheet could melt and sea-levels would rise, flooding many low-lying areas.

greenhouse gases

carbon dioxide

CFCs

methane

Greenhouse gases
Carbon dioxide is responsible for 49 per cent of the extra warming, methane 18 per cent, CFCs 14 per cent, nitrous oxides 6 per cent and others, mostly ozone in the lower atmosphere, 13 per cent.

Carbon dioxide is released into the atmosphere when fossil fuels or wood are burnt. Growing trees take in carbon dioxide, and so the destruction of huge areas of forest adds to the amount of carbon dioxide in the atmosphere.

Methane is produced by rotting plant and animal material from paddy fields, gas given off by cattle, waste dumps and termites, and leaks in natural gas pipelines.

Right Burning fossil fuels in power stations is a major source of carbon dioxide.

CFCs from aerosol sprays, fridges and air conditioners evaporate and find their way into the atmosphere.

Nitrous oxides come from agricultural fertilizers and vehicle exhaust emissions, and ozone is also produced by vehicle exhausts.

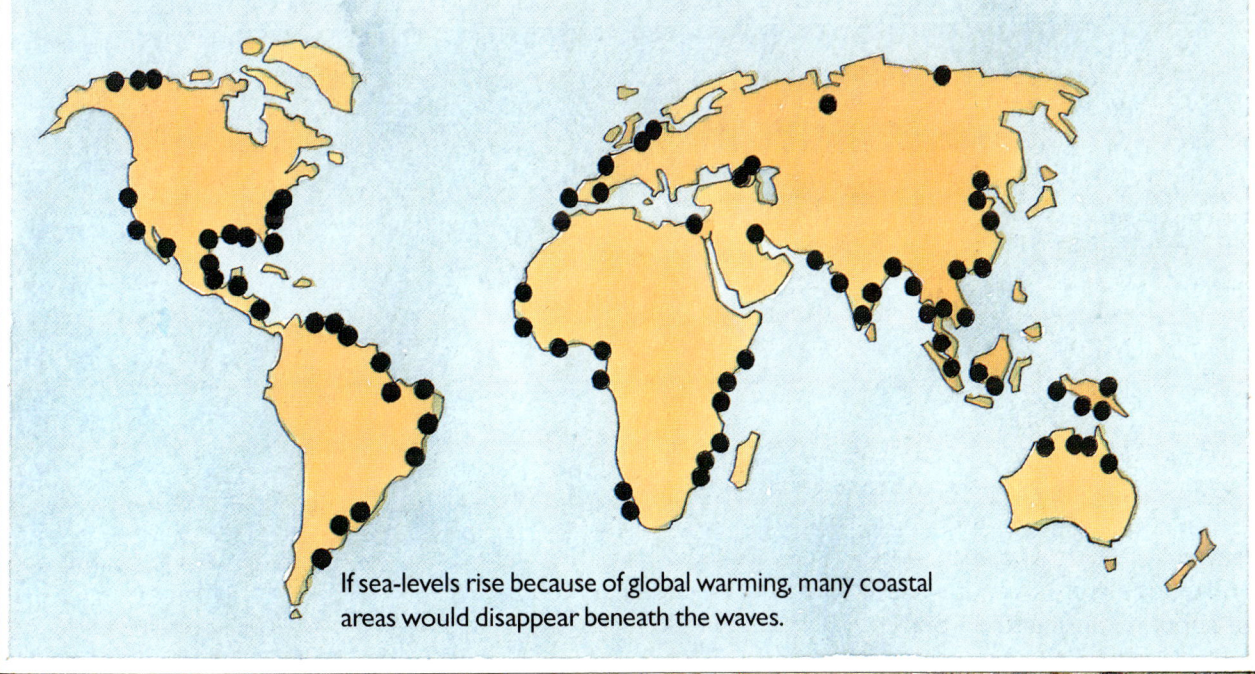

carbon dioxide absorbed by trees

If sea-levels rise because of global warming, many coastal areas would disappear beneath the waves.

GREENHOUSE EFFECT — 2

Turning Down the Heat

The whole planet will be affected by global warming although it is the world's richest nations that add most of the extra carbon dioxide to the atmosphere. No single country can solve the problems by itself — international co-operation is needed. Organizations such as the United Nations Environment Programme and the World Conservation Union bring together people from all countries to try and solve international environmental problems.

The idea of Gaia
Astronauts in their spaceships need to take their fuel, air, food and water with them. The only thing they do not have to take is the energy they can collect from the sun using solar panels. The earth is like a spaceship on an endless journey through space, and it has no chance to stop off anywhere to collect fresh supplies.

Unlike spaceships, the earth has developed ways of providing all its plant and animal inhabitants with the necessary supplies for their journey by recycling and cleaning the air, the water and the soil. Together all the processes taking place seem to have one purpose — to create the best conditions for life to flourish.

The scientist James Lovelock called this regenerating process Gaia, after the Greek goddess who symbolized the earth. We humans are part of nature but are damaging some of the planet's major systems that enable life to succeed. Lovelock's idea is that we should try and work with the forces of nature rather than try to overcome them.

Solar panels in Senegal, Africa. Alternative energy sources do not produce greenhouse gases.

The carbon cycle

Carbon is one of the elements that make up the earth. It exists in the atmosphere as carbon dioxide. Through the process of photosynthesis plants in the sea and on land manufacture carbohydrates from carbon dioxide. Carbon is returned to the atmosphere as carbon dioxide by animals when they breathe and when living material dies and decays. Some carbon remains stored in dead material that is buried, such as coal, and is only released when the coal is burnt.

Right This diagram shows the natural cycle of carbon in the environment.

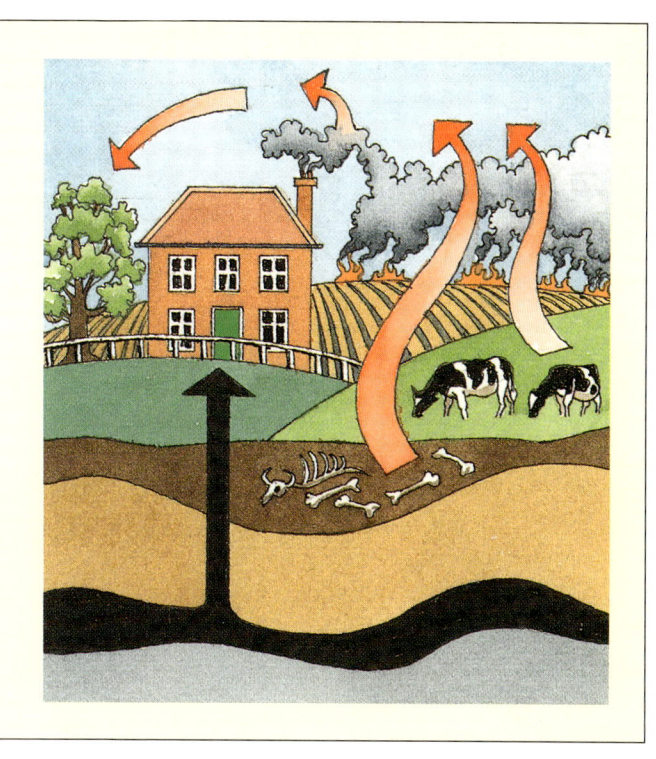

Solving the problem

There are a number of ways in which global warming can be slowed down or halted. Some chemicals, such as CFCs, can be replaced by less damaging ones or not be used at all. Deodorants and cleaning materials, for example, can be used in solid form rather than as an aerosol spray.

Cleaner fuels can be used: natural gas produces only half as much carbon dioxide as other fossil fuels do in supplying the same amount of energy.

By designing engines, washing machines, refrigerators, light bulbs and other devices so that they use less energy, fewer fossil fuels need be burnt. This is called energy efficiency.

Alternative sources of energy, including the wind, waves and the sun, do not produce any greenhouse gases, and so the more we use these sources the better.

Planting trees helps to reduce the amount of carbon dioxide in the atmosphere. One American company has agreed to plant 52 million trees in Guatemala, Central America, to absorb the carbon dioxide from a new power station it is building. Stopping the destruction of forests would also help.

What you can do
Try to use as little energy as possible. For example, turn off the lights and heaters when they are not needed. Look around your home and school to see how energy could be saved.

THE OZONE LAYER — 1

A Hole in the Sky

Energy from the sun and the atmosphere make it possible for living things to survive on earth. However, the sun's ultraviolet (UV) rays can damage living things. For example, humans can suffer from sunburn and skin cancer.

Between about 20 and 25 kilometres up in the atmosphere, there is a layer of ozone gas that screens out almost all these harmful UV rays. Some years ago, the British Antarctic Survey discovered that the ozone layer was being damaged. They found that the amount of ozone over Antarctica decreases alarmingly during the spring but recovers naturally later in the year. The ozone hole had been discovered.

Satellites and aeroplanes now monitor the ozone layer continuously. The hole above the Antarctic can grow as large as North America and spread over southern Australia. At the centre of the hole 98 per cent of the ozone has been lost. A thinning of the ozone layer has also been found above the Arctic. Elsewhere the loss of ozone is smaller, but a loss of 7 per cent of the ozone is already experienced over half of Britain and parts of North America.

This satellite picture of the earth shows the levels of ozone in the atmosphere in the southern hemisphere. The white and dark blue areas are those where the ozone layer is thinnest.

Radiation damage to life
Even a tiny increase in the amount of UV reaching the surface can damage living things. For humans, the increase will cause more skin cancers and eye cataracts.

Plants exposed to UV grow less well. Microscopic plants in the ocean, called phytoplankton, are the basis of a food chain that supports all kinds of marine life. Phytoplankton living near the surface of the Antarctic Ocean have already been damaged.

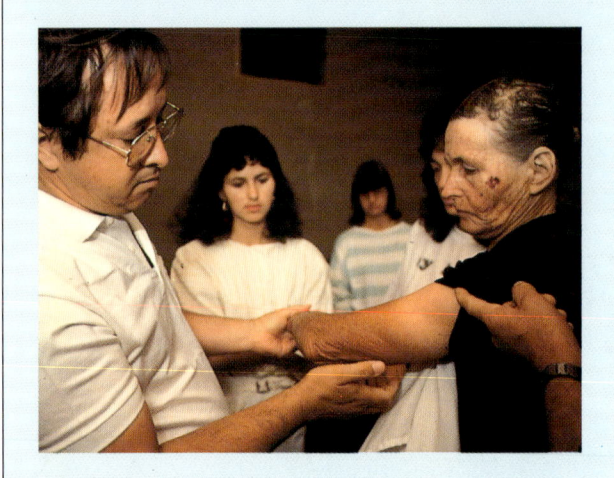

Above Doctors in Brazil examine a patient with skin cancer.

The ozone eaters

The major cause of the present problem is a chemical element called chlorine, which is found in a group of chemicals called chlorofluorocarbons (CFCs). Once released, CFCs drift into the upper atmosphere, often taking several years to do so. Ultraviolet light then breaks up the CFCs and the chlorine is released. When chlorine and ozone meet, the ozone is converted into oxygen.

CFCs are cheap, do not burn, and are not poisonous. Nevertheless, they are destroying the ozone layer. About 1.2 million tonnes of CFCs are produced each year, to clean electrical components, drive liquids as a spray out of aerosols, make foam packaging like the cartons used by fast-food shops, and for use in refrigerators and air conditioners.

The ozone layer is also damaged by carbon tetrachloride and methyl chloroform, both of which are cleaning fluids. Chemicals called halons, which contain ozone-destroying bromine, are used for putting out fires. Countries such as Australia rely on them for fighting bush fires. Nitrous oxides, methane and fluorine also help destroy the ozone layer.

CFCs are broken apart by the sun's ultraviolet rays, and this produces atoms of chlorine. The chlorine atoms react with ozone, again producing chlorine atoms. As this process continues, more ozone is destroyed, allowing more ultraviolet rays to reach the earth.

THE OZONE LAYER — 2

Patching the Ozone Hole

Even if all CFCs were banned today, there are so many in the atmosphere already that it would take 50 years for the ozone layer over Antarctica to return to what it was in the early 1970s. Scientists have known about the damage that CFCs can cause for some time. The USA banned the use of CFCs in aerosols in 1978, a decision that has lost American industry about US$1.5 billion.

Today more countries and industries are using substitutes that do not damage the ozone layer. McDonalds, the giant fast-food chain, has agreed not to sell take-away food in foam containers made using CFCs; Dupont, one of the world's biggest chemical companies, is not using so many CFCs; and the computer company IBM is finding new chemicals to clean the electrical parts used in its products. It is now possible to buy aerosols that carry an 'ozone friendly' symbol. These usually contain butane, which does not damage the ozone layer, instead of CFCs. However, butane is a greenhouse gas and will add further to the greenhouse effect. Sprays that are worked by a simple handpump do not damage the ozone layer or cause global warming.

The Montreal Protocol
In September 1987, forty-six countries signed the Montreal Protocol, an agreement to cut the use of some ozone-destroying chemicals by 50 per cent by the year 1999. But as the seriousness of the problem became more apparent, the Environmental Protection Agency in the USA said that a 100 per cent reduction would be needed to save the ozone layer. In May 1989, some eighty-one nations agreed to strengthen the Montreal Protocol and ban CFCs by 2000.

Britain is the largest producer of CFCs in Europe, and the largest exporter of them. It exports most of its CFCs to countries that have refused to sign the Montreal Protocol.

Public campaigns

Very few aerosols for sale today contain CFCs. In 1988, the environmental group Friends of the Earth launched a campaign to stop their use. They produced information for schools, the public and industry about the damage CFCs were doing to the ozone layer. They also produced a list of aerosols that did not contain CFCs. This helped people to choose 'ozone friendly' products in the shop. The campaign received a lot of publicity on television and in the newspapers. Many people refused to buy aerosols containing CFCs, and so manufacturers stopped making them.

Above In April 1990, Greenpeace protesters demonstrated at an ICI chemicals plant in Runcorn, England, where CFCs are manufactured.

Left There are alternatives to products that contain CFCs — handpump sprays and recycled paper containers are as effective as aerosols and foam boxes.

What you can do
Avoid buying aerosols, especially those that are not labelled 'ozone friendly'. Buy pump-action containers instead, or use air fresheners and deodorants that are in solid form. Don't buy take-away food in foam containers.

ACID RAIN — 1

Poisoning the Environment

When fossil fuels such as coal, oil and natural gas are burnt, fumes are produced. Although they are known to be poisonous, these fumes are pushed out into the atmosphere through power station and factory chimneys and vehicle exhaust pipes. The air dilutes them and the wind blows them away, but they do not become harmless.

Moisture in the air absorbs sulphur dioxide and nitrogen oxides contained in the fumes. These chemicals turn the moisture in the air to acid. It can then fall to the ground as rain, snow or mist.

Acid rain damages the environment. Lakes are normally full of life, but in Scandinavia and Canada some lakes are so acid that hardly anything lives in them — they are dead. Trees are dying in forests throughout Europe before they can grow large enough to be cut for timber. Some farmland is becoming less fertile. When the acid rain soaks into the soil it can release metals such as aluminium which can get into the water we drink. High levels of aluminium are thought to cause Alzheimer's disease, a condition in which people suffer severe loss of memory.

Too many cars?
There are about 550 million vehicles in the world, enough to make a traffic jam stretching forty times around the earth. In Britain 5,500 new cars are registered each day to add to the 20 million already on the road. Air pollution in big cities is mainly caused by traffic.

Pollution from vehicle exhausts comes in several forms. Carbon monoxide interferes with the supply of oxygen to the brain causing dizziness and headaches. Hydrocarbons in unburnt fuel and nitrogen oxides react with strong sunlight to form ozone. In the upper levels of the atmosphere, ozone screens the earth from harmful ultraviolet rays, but closer to the earth it is a poison that irritates the eyes and lungs. Carbon dioxide adds to the greenhouse effect. Lead from cars not using lead-free petrol can cause brain damage in children. Soot and smoke from diesel engines which are not adjusted properly can cause cancer.

Main picture Sulphur dioxide and nitrogen oxides from vehicle exhausts and burning fossil fuels mix with moisture in the air to form acid.

sulphur dioxide and nitrogen oxides

smoke from homes and factories

vehicle exhaust fumes

Damage to buildings
Acid rain eats into metal and stonework and adds to the cost of keeping buildings safe and looking good. The stonework on many famous old buildings, such as the Parthenon in Greece, has been damaged more by pollution in the atmosphere during the last 70 years than in all the years since they were built. In 1984 the Statue of Liberty in New York, USA, had to be restored because it had corroded so much.

Left and right A statue in Lincoln, England, before and after the effects of acid rain.

ACID RAIN — 2

The Road to Recovery

What you can do
Save energy and cut down on pollution by walking, cycling or travelling on public transport whenever possible. If your parents have a car, ask them to buy lead-free petrol and, if necessary, have a catalytic converter fitted.

There is now an international agreement to reduce the amount of sulphur dioxide getting into the atmosphere. Also, in 1988, several European countries agreed to reduce nitrogen oxide emissions by 1995. Vehicle exhaust fumes are one of the main causes of these types of pollution, and some countries have recently brought in their own laws to try and reduce them. The USA has set very strict controls called the US83 Standard, and this has been adopted as a target by several other countries including Austria, Switzerland, Norway and Sweden. The standard first set by the European Community (EC), the Euronorm, was much less strict, but in 1989 the EC agreed to impose US-style exhaust standards by 1992.

A catalytic converter can reduce a car's hydrocarbon and nitrogen oxide emissions by 90 per cent, but it will only work if lead-free petrol is used.

To reach the standard, most cars need to be fitted with a catalytic converter. Some car companies are now producing so-called 'lean-burn' engines which burn fuel more efficiently and create less pollution. Other fuels are also being used. The fumes from alcohol-driven cars in Brazil are almost clean enough to breathe.

Catalytic converters

A catalytic converter is a small device fitted into the exhaust of a car. It converts the harmful gases into carbon dioxide, nitrogen and water. Catalytic converters use very expensive rare metals and add about 5 per cent to the cost of a new car. Some car manufacturers are now fitting them to their most popular models. In Germany almost half of all new cars are now fitted with converters.

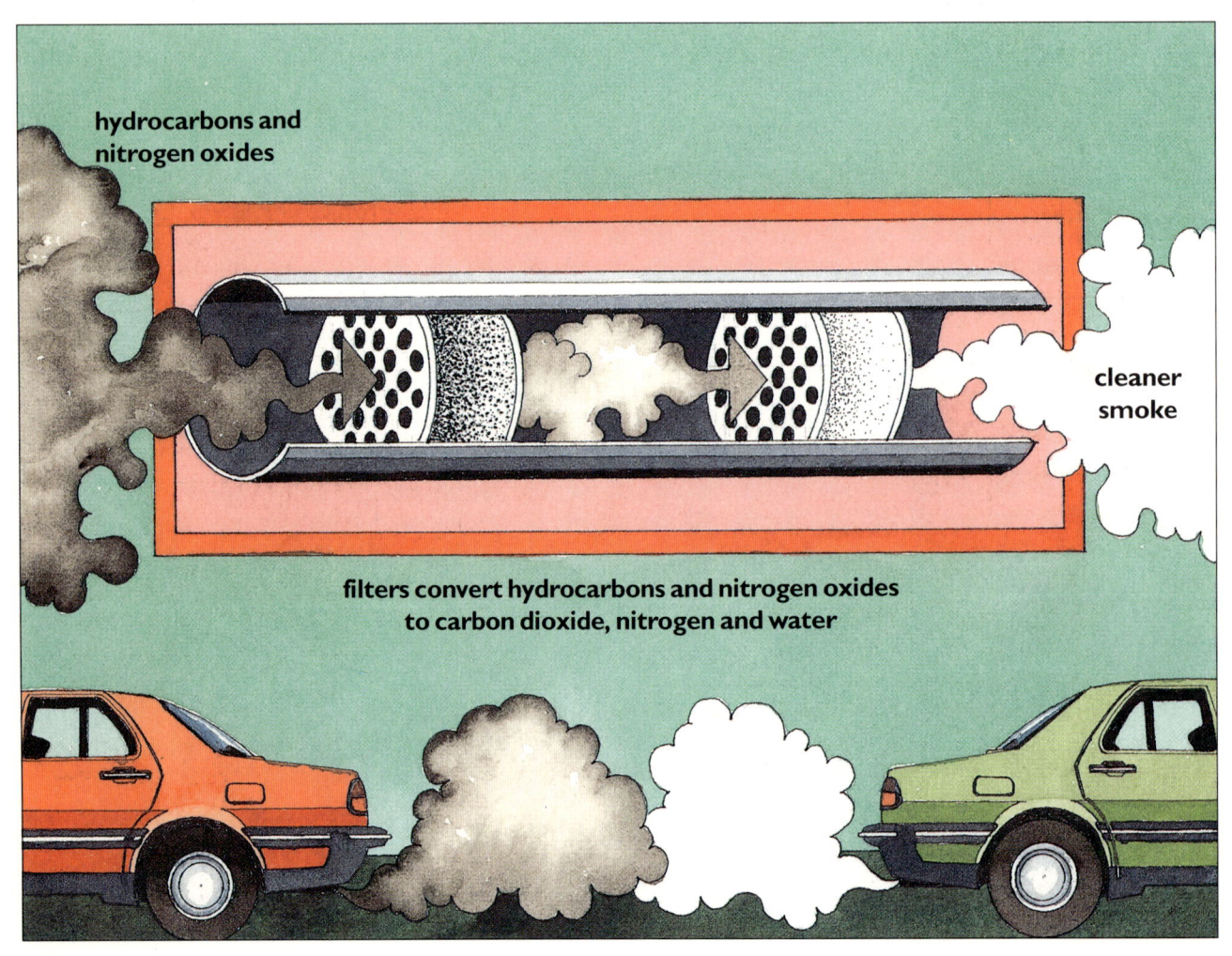

hydrocarbons and nitrogen oxides

cleaner smoke

filters convert hydrocarbons and nitrogen oxides to carbon dioxide, nitrogen and water

Public transport

Many pollution problems are caused by the sheer number of vehicles, especially cars, in use today. The problems are worst in cities. The amount of pollution would be reduced if more people used public transport instead of private cars. One bus can carry about 70 people, a tram about 100 and a train 1,000. In contrast, a car can carry only 4 or 5 people.

Some cities are improving their public transport systems. Many towns in Britain have bus lanes so that the buses avoid traffic jams. In Cologne, Germany, it is possible for passengers to change easily between trains, trams and buses which run on routes separate from cars. The government in the Netherlands planned to cut air pollution by reducing the number of cars on the road from 5 million to 3.5 million and improving public transport. New taxes were to be introduced to increase the cost of owning and running a car. However, the scheme met so much opposition that the plans were not put into action.

More than 100,000 street parking places in Paris, France, are being removed as part of a plan to allow only public transport and pedestrians to enter much of the city.

Above Trains, buses and trams cause less pollution per passenger than cars.

Below Many of the vehicles in this traffic jam are carrying only one person.

NUCLEAR ENERGY — 1

A Nuclear Future?

The shattered nuclear reactor after the explosion at Chernobyl, and the spread of the radioactive cloud it created.

The world is facing an energy crisis. Most of the energy we use comes from fossil fuels such as coal, oil and natural gas. These fuels pollute the atmosphere when they are burnt, and they are being used at such a fast rate that they will eventually become scarce and run out.

Electricity can be generated using the energy that is released when an atom is split. This is known as nuclear energy. The easiest atom to split is found in uranium; 1 tonne of uranium will generate as much electricity as 20,000 tonnes of coal without

farm crops contaminated

towns and villages around Chernobyl abandoned

sheep meat in Britain found to be radioactive

reindeer in northern Scandinavia and Lappland affected

causing the same pollution problems. However, radiation from nuclear fuel and waste can be dangerous. A large dose can kill a person in a few days, but even a very small dose can cause cancers.

Chernobyl

No nuclear power station can be completely safe, and there have been accidents. The worst was in 1986 at Chernobyl in the USSR, where a huge explosion and fire in a nuclear power station sent a cloud of radioactive gases and dust into the atmosphere. Radiation in the area was so high that people living within 30 kilometres of the reactor had to leave their homes permanently. The radioactive cloud spread over much of Europe and reached parts of North America. Three years later, farmers in some parts of Britain were still not allowed to sell their sheep because the meat was considered too radioactive to be eaten safely. This disaster convinced many people that the risks of nuclear power are so great that we should stop producing it altogether.

Refugees leaving the Chernobyl area are checked to see how much radiation they have received.

The economics of energy

The modern world cannot do without electricity. What is the best method of producing this electricity cheaply and safely without damaging the environment? There is no single answer, but there are several choices.

- Coal and oil are relatively cheap and very reliable but both cause serious pollution problems. They will also get more expensive as they become rarer.
- Nuclear power is expensive. There is little pollution when power stations are working properly, but a serious accident can be devastating and very costly.
- Hydroelectric power is cheaper and very reliable and causes no pollution. The only 'fuel' used is rainwater. Lakes behind hydroelectric dams can flood sensitive environments and not all countries have suitable sites.
- Wind, wave, tidal, solar and geothermal power will never run out, but the methods used to generate them are still in their early stages. Some schemes take up huge areas of land or sea and are not very attractive to look at. However, recent surveys have shown that most people would rather live close to a wind generator, for example, than a power station.

NUCLEAR ENERGY — 2

Energy Saving

As we have seen, there are many ways of generating electricity. Anyone who has struggled against a strong head-wind on a bicycle has experienced the energy in the wind, and sailors have used this source of energy for centuries. Energy in sunlight, the wind, waves, waterfalls, tides and hot rocks below the ground can be used to make electricity.

To date, only the energy in falling water is being widely used as an alternative to using fossil or nuclear fuels in power stations. This is called hydroelectric power, and it accounts for about 20 per cent of all the electricity produced in the world. Electricity is generated when water collected behind a dam is carried downhill through a pipe to turn a turbine which generates electricity. Mountainous areas with plenty of rainfall, such as Norway, are ideal for building hydroelectric power stations.

Here are some of the ways in which houses can be designed or modified so that they use less energy. It is also possible to design and build domestic appliances, such as refrigerators and washing machines, to use less electricity.

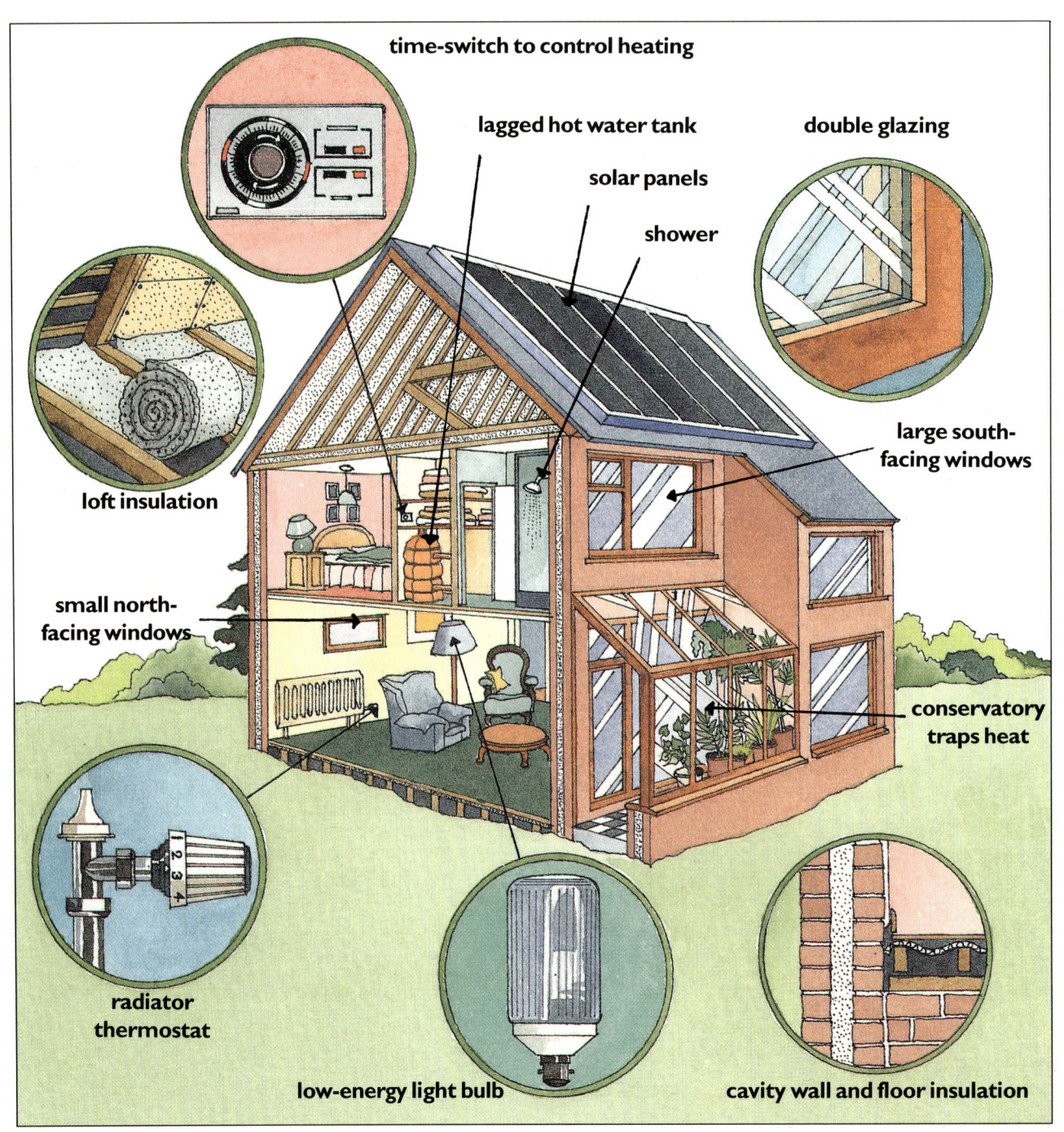

- time-switch to control heating
- lagged hot water tank
- solar panels
- shower
- double glazing
- large south-facing windows
- loft insulation
- small north-facing windows
- conservatory traps heat
- radiator thermostat
- low-energy light bulb
- cavity wall and floor insulation

Geothermal promise
Rocks under the ground are hot, sometimes so hot that they melt. In some parts of the world this molten rock is pushed up towards the surface and may erupt as a volcano. In Iceland, where there is a lot of volcanic activity, water under the ground is heated by the rocks. This hot water is used to heat homes, offices, factories and greenhouses.

Even where there is no volcanic activity water can be pumped into the earth where it becomes very hot. It can then be pumped back to the surface and used to heat buildings or generate electricity.

Above A geothermal energy station in Iceland.

Below The Hoover Dam in Arizona, USA. The energy of falling water can be used to produce electricity without causing great pollution problems.

Reducing our energy needs
All methods of generating electricity change the environment in some way, even if only slightly. It therefore makes sense to use as little energy as possible so that fewer new power stations are needed, pollution and damage to the environment will not increase so fast, and fuels such as coal and oil will last longer.

In the home, energy can be saved by putting in proper insulation, such as glassfibre in the roof, foam between the inside and outside walls, double glazing, tight-fitting doors and windows, and fitted carpets. Taking a shower instead of a bath also uses less energy.

When you are travelling, public transport can carry you much further on a litre of fuel than a motor car. For short distances, walking or cycling is even better.

What you can do
The less electricity you use the less fuel will have to be consumed to produce it. A shower uses less hot water than a bath, for example. Ask your parents to make sure that your home is properly insulated.

RADIOACTIVE WASTE — 1

Waste Not Wanted

Nuclear power is one source of electrical energy. It provides some of the power we need to heat and light our homes, cook, and run factories and offices. In Britain, it provides about 7 per cent of the electricity we use. However, its waste products are dangerous because they are radioactive. This means that they give off particles, or 'rays', which can damage the living cells of humans and other animals. Large doses of radioactivity can cause cancer by destroying healthy cells, but small doses of radioactivity are used in hospitals to kill cancer cells in the body.

Radioactivity fades, or decays, with time, although some radioactive materials, such as plutonium and uranium, take millions of years to decay to a safe level. So radioactive waste has to be dealt with very carefully so as not to damage life on the earth, now or in the future.

Used nuclear fuel can be reprocessed at plants such as this one in Sellafield, England, to make new fuel. However, the waste left behind after reprocessing is extremely radioactive.

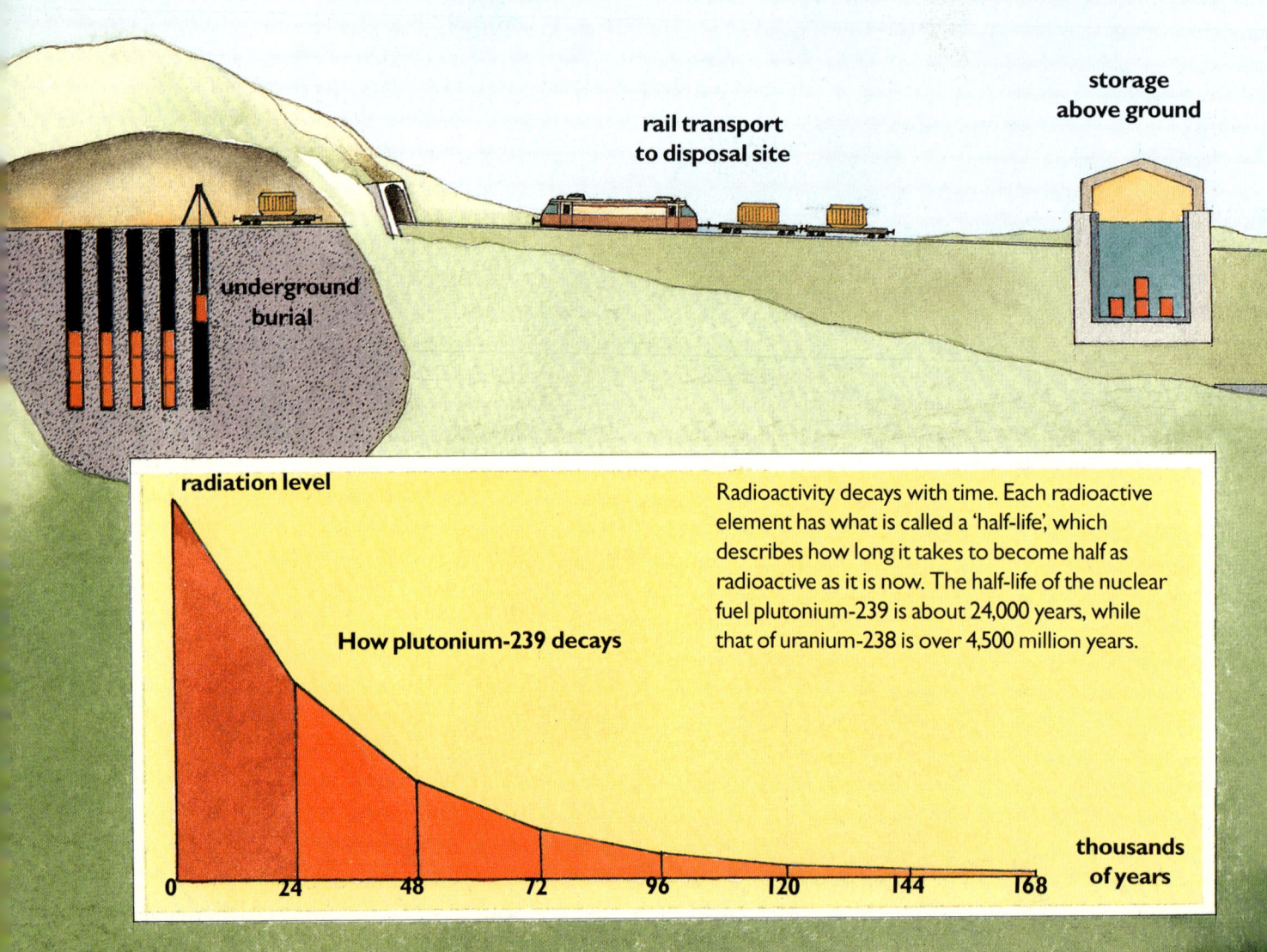

underground burial

rail transport to disposal site

storage above ground

How plutonium-239 decays

radiation level

0   24   48   72   96   120   144   168   thousands of years

Radioactivity decays with time. Each radioactive element has what is called a 'half-life', which describes how long it takes to become half as radioactive as it is now. The half-life of the nuclear fuel plutonium-239 is about 24,000 years, while that of uranium-238 is over 4,500 million years.

Disposal and storage

Wastes are described as being low, intermediate- or high-level and they are disposed of in different ways. Solid, low-level waste is buried underground at disposal sites, gases are pumped into the atmosphere, and liquid waste is released into the sea. Intermediate-level waste is more dangerous and cannot be released into the environment. It is currently stored in concrete containers at special sites at nuclear power stations. The most dangerous waste, high-level waste, is usually stored at nuclear stations in cooling tanks full of water.

How radioactive?

- Low-level waste decays quickly and is low in radioactivity. It includes contaminated rubbish, used protective clothing and equipment from hospitals, universities and nuclear power stations.
- Intermediate-level waste is more concentrated and includes solid waste such as containers used for transporting radioactive materials, other equipment and radioactive sludge produced by the nuclear power and weapons industries.
- High-level waste is the most dangerous type of waste and may take millions of years to decay. It includes used fuel rods and liquid waste from nuclear power stations.

Main picture Nuclear power stations allow radioactivity to enter the environment around them. They also produce radioactive waste which has to be stored. In the past, some waste was dumped at sea.

radioactivity into the environment

nuclear power station

road transport to disposal site

sea dumping

undersea burial

RADIOACTIVE WASTE — 2

Not in My Backyard

There is a great deal of opposition to the use of nuclear power and to the transport and disposal of radioactive waste. Many people are worried about nuclear waste and fear it may affect their health, particularly if it is disposed of near their homes.

In 1983, NIREX (Nuclear Industry Radioactive Research Executive) the government organization that is responsible for low- and intermediate-level waste in Britain, announced that it was considering Billingham in Cleveland and Elstow in Bedfordshire as possible sites to bury wastes. The people of Billingham and Elstow were united in their determination not to allow nuclear waste near their homes. They formed pressure groups and campaigned strongly by protesting to their local councillors and Members of Parliament. They wrote to local and national newspapers and publicized their campaign on radio and television. They organized demonstrations and blocked entrances to the proposed sites. Nuclear waste dumping became a national issue. Faced with such a display of 'people power', NIREX eventually withdrew its plans for the dumps. NIREX proposed another site near Bradwell, in Essex. But local opposition was so strong that the plan was dropped in 1986.

Can waste be safe?

However, radioactive waste exists and has to be disposed of somewhere. There are various ways of looking at the problem, and several possible solutions.

Environmental organizations such as Greenpeace and Friends of the Earth say that the only responsible method of handling the waste is to keep

When NIREX announced their plan for a low-level nuclear waste dump near Bradwell, England, local people protested successfully against it.

warm air out

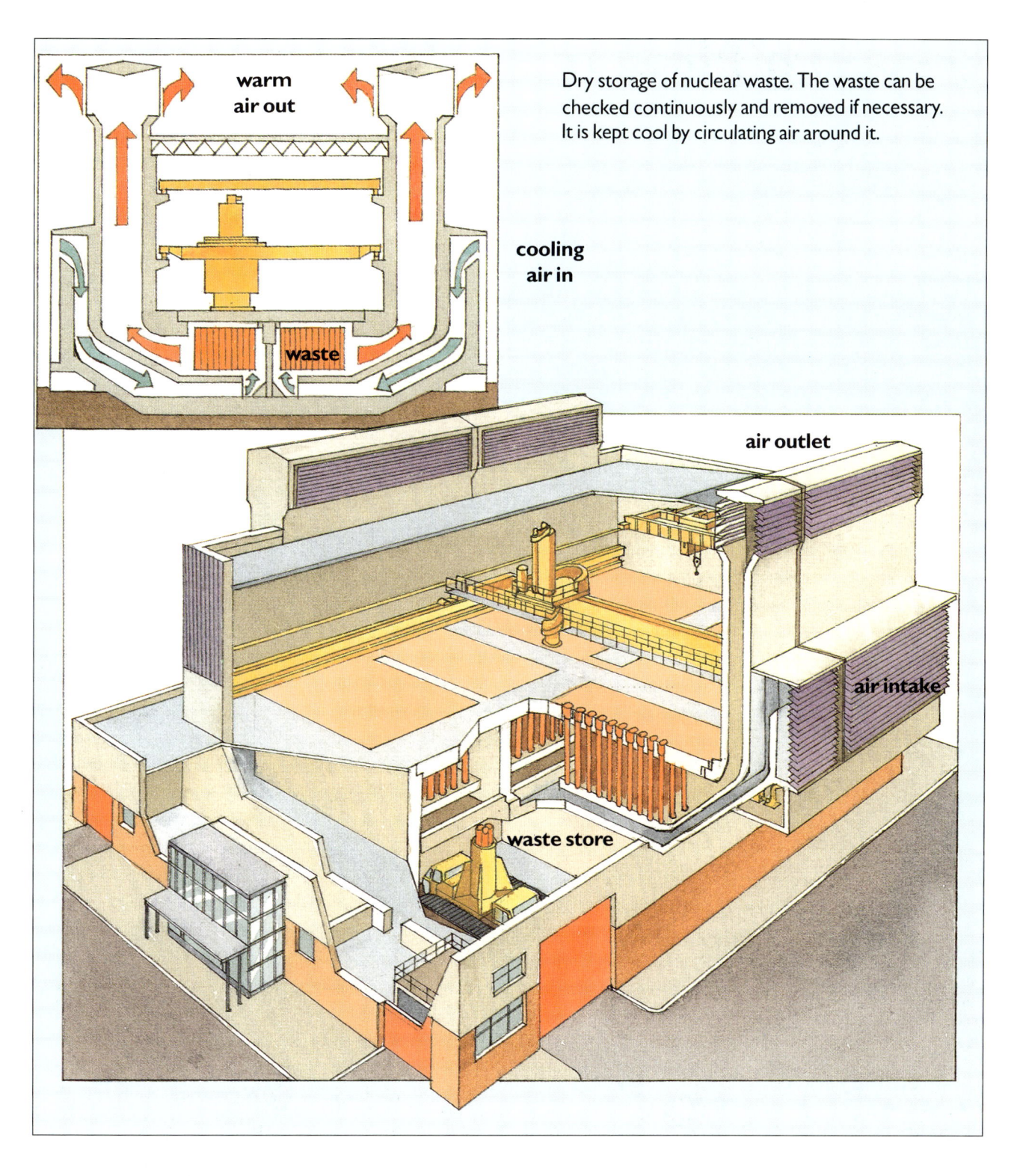

cooling air in

waste

Dry storage of nuclear waste. The waste can be checked continuously and removed if necessary. It is kept cool by circulating air around it.

air outlet

air intake

waste store

it in special 'dry storage' facilities at the power stations where it is produced. This has the advantage that the waste can be monitored regularly, and it does not need to be transported from place to place.

NIREX and government organizations in other countries are looking for new ways of disposing nuclear waste. Their latest suggestion is that it should be buried in deep underground sites. Some environmentalists say that the radioactivity may seep out eventually and contaminate the environment.

Perhaps the best solution to the radioactive waste problem is to produce less of it. The waste that already exists will not go away but it is possible to stop creating more. Conserving energy by using it carefully and without wasting it is one solution. Developing renewable sources such as wind, wave, tidal and solar power may be another way of reducing the waste. (See pages 18 to 21.)

CULTURE LOSS — 1

Vanishing Tribes

There are about 200 million tribal people living in the world today, making up about 14 per cent of the world's population. Tribal peoples are groups who have their own society and traditions — art, music, religion, language and legends — and who are self-supporting. They live by hunting, herding, farming or fishing, and are found all over the world. Australian Aborigines, the Bushmen of the Kalahari Desert in Africa and South American indians are all tribal peoples.

Buffalo hunting

The threats to tribal people

Many tribes have been victims of other races and societies who have invaded or colonized their land. Very often the invaders were white men who came from Europe, or had European-style societies. Indian people first came to North America 50,000 years ago. Over the years they colonized the whole continent and developed their own ways of life. Between 1520 and 1890 they fought the European settlers who were taking their land and destroying

Invaders from Europe

The Yanomami

Indian societies have lived in South America for 20,000 years, but in the sixteenth century their way of life was changed by the Spanish conquest. There were about 14 million Indians in South America at that time, but their populations decreased rapidly as the Europeans killed many of them. Others were taken as slaves or died from disease. Some escaped into more remote areas.

The Yanomami tribe live in the Amazon area of Brazil and Venezuela. They know how to live successfully in the tropical rainforest, which foods to eat and which plants are medicines. Today there about 14,500 Yanomami. They are the largest tribe left in South America but they are on the brink of being destroyed forever. The rich resources of the Amazon, especially gold, have attracted over 50,000 miners. Neither the miners nor the Brazilian government respects the Yanomami's land and there have been many violent clashes. Many Yanomami have been murdered and whole villages have been burnt. The future for this tribe looks bleak.

Above Yanomami Indians in the Amazon rainforest of Brazil.

their unique culture. It was a battle they lost and most tribes had to leave their homeland and give up their traditional lifestyle. Tribes and their way of life have been destroyed by mining, road building, forestry and by religious missionaries or tourists. The invaders have taken tribal lands, made slaves of the people, murdered them and infected them with diseases to which they have no resistance. This has gone on for centuries and tribes are still being threatened today. In Indonesia, government policies of economic development are threatening 2 million tribal people. The government wants to move them from their land and re-educate them so that they will become what the government calls 'normal communities'.

Main picture American Indians first lived in North America 50,000 years ago. White settlers began arriving about 500 years ago, since when many Indians have been killed or driven from their land on to reservations.

Indian wars

A reservation

CULTURE LOSS — 2

Survival Against the Odds

Many tribes are destroyed in the name of progress. The invaders see tribal peoples as primitive and isolated from civilization. They seek to modernize the tribes and to make them 'normal'. What the invaders do not see is that tribal societies are stable and self-supporting. The people in them are not backward but have a unique knowledge of their environment. They know how to live off the land without destroying it. They have their own traditions which are as valuable as any others. Above all, they have a right to their way of life.

Many tribal people are beginning to claim their rights. They are defending their land, traditions and societies against other cultures. Two groups, the Inuit (Eskimo) people of the Arctic and the Australian Aborigines, have had some success in their fight to have their rights recognized by others, to be able to live in their traditional lands and to determine their own future. It is a difficult task. The tribes need national and international support and organization to help them survive.

More and more stories of the plight of tribal peoples are reaching newspapers around the world. People are supporting their cause and international organizations are working for them and with them.

Tribal peoples are well adapted to their environment and know how to use it without destroying it.

Australian Aborigines — fighting back

The Aborigines have lived in Australia for 40,000 years. Their traditions and way of life are centred on the land. The invasion of white Europeans, which began in 1788, destroyed much of their land and culture but the Aborigines are fighting back. In the last 50 years they have organized themselves. They set up the Land Rights Campaign and demanded the return and protection of their land and sacred sites. They also called for the right to determine their own future. The situation is hopeful: there is now a Minister for Aboriginal Affairs in the government. Aborigines can vote and they are being given back some of their land including Ayers Rock, one of their most sacred sites, in central Australia.

Below Australian Aborigines demanding the return of lands taken from them by whites.

Survival International

Survival International is an organization that works for the rights of threatened tribal peoples. It does not want to preserve them as though they were in a museum or a zoo. Instead, it tries to ensure their future and allow them to adapt to the changing world in their own way. Survival International campaigns for change, publicizes cases and educates people about threatened tribes.

What you can do

Choose a traditional or tribal people such as the Inuit or Aborigines. Try to find out about their way of life and compare it with your own. Do you think one is better than the other, or are they just different? Try to respect other people's right to live according to their own culture.

WASTE AND POLLUTION — 1

Our Polluted World

Waste is slowly poisoning the earth. Chemicals and metals used in industrial processes, pesticides, sewage, agricultural and domestic waste are all dumped into the environment. The waste is mainly from the developed or Western countries, which manufacture and consume most of the world's products and resources.

Solid and liquid waste is often dumped in holes in the ground called landfill sites. Some liquid waste is released into rivers and seas. Waste is also burnt or incinerated, sometimes in ocean incinerator ships. This is a highly technical process — for example PCBs (polychlorinated biphenyls) have to be burnt at 1,100°C. PCBs are known to be a possible cause of cancers and nervous illnesses. They have been used in a number of industrial processes but are now banned. However, quantities of PCBs still exist and there are different opinions on how to dispose of them safely. Some people say that if they are incinerated properly there are no harmful by-products, but many environmentalists disagree.

industrial pollution

liquid waste

partially treated sewage

pesticide spraying

Hazardous cargoes

The developed countries also dispose of their waste by exporting it, usually to developing countries where safety regulations are less strict. Toxic waste travels the world through the seas and the air. It pollutes the world's environments and enters the food chains as animals eat one another, and eventually finds its way back to humans. Traces of chemicals from Europe and North America have been found in the Antarctic ice and in animals such as seals and whales.

incinerator ship

dumping at sea

landfill site

agricultural fertilizer

The case of the *Karin B*

In 1988 the *Karin B* sailed the seas looking for a port that would accept her cargo of 167 containers (about 3,500 tonnes) of toxic waste — PCBs, drugs, solvents, acids and pesticides. The waste came from Italy and was first dumped illegally in Nigeria, where the leaking containers were left within 140 metres of a village water supply. In Europe it would cost £2,000 per tonne to dispose of wastes but in Nigeria it cost only £60 per month to store them. However, Nigeria ordered the removal of the containers and the *Karin B* was hired to take the waste back to Italy. When Italy refused it entry, the *Karin B* then sailed to ports in five other European countries but none allowed it in. Eventually the ship was forced to take its dangerous load back to Italy.

Above The *Karin B* during its search for somewhere to unload its deadly cargo.

Main picture Toxic waste enters the environment in a variety of ways. Pollution from industry, agriculture and our homes finds its way into the air, soil, rivers and the sea. Most of this waste is produced by the world's developed countries. Dumping the waste is cheaper than treating it to make it safe.

Cut Down, Clean Up

What alternatives are there to dumping or burning waste? Many environmental groups say that if we consumed less products there would be less waste of all kinds. Rather than trying to deal with more and more waste, it must make sense to produce less of it in the first place. About 85 per cent of the world's resources are consumed by 25 per cent of the world's population, mainly in the developed countries. To consume less would mean changing the way we live — using less packaging, less energy, fewer cars, videos, fridges and other consumer goods. It would also mean re-using and recycling materials rather than throwing them away.

Consumer power

Some supermarkets and local authorities now encourage recycling by putting bottle and metal can banks in their car parks. The glass and metal is then melted down and used to make new bottles and cans. In Denmark, 99 per cent of all bottles are now collected and refilled. Recyclable plastics, such as PET, have been developed recently but, as yet,

Most of the waste that we throw out could be re-used or recycled, which would save valuable resources, cut down on the energy we use and reduce pollution.

| glass 10% | metal 10% | organic 30% | paper 30% | miscellaneous 12% | plastic 8% |

What do we throw out?

Action on PCBs

In August 1989, Greenpeace volunteers in inflatable dinghies attached a skull and cross bones flag to a Russian cargo ship at Tilbury Docks in London. This was to draw attention to the import of toxic PCBs into Britain. Greenpeace persuaded dock workers and port managers at Tilbury to turn away the shipment. The Port of Liverpool then announced it would refuse a consignment of 15 shiploads of PCBs from Canada destined for incineration at the ReChem plant in Pontypool, South Wales, the world's largest importer of PCB waste. The Transport and General Workers' Union said it would support any dock workers who refused to unload the ship. Ports around the country refused to take the shipment.

Despite opposition from port managers, dockers, local residents and environmental groups, the government refused to intervene, saying the shipments were part of a normal commercial transaction. In the government's view, the import and disposal of toxic waste, when professionally handled, is ecologically safe and helps the economy. In 1987, the UK imported 83,000 tonnes of dangerous wastes like these.

Rather than spread PCBs further and wider in the environment through transportation and incineration, Greenpeace favours storing them above ground, where they can be monitored and retrieved, until such time as a truly safe way exists to break them down into harmless by-products.

Greenpeace wants a total world-wide ban on shipments of hazardous waste to force the producer countries to think seriously about reducing the amount of toxic waste they create.

Bottle banks like these are now a familiar sight in many cities. The glass is collected, melted down and made into new bottles.

there are few schemes to handle their collection and processing. As in the case of CFC-free products (see page 13), if enough consumers demand re-usable and recyclable products and refuse to buy those that aren't, manufacturers will be forced to produce them.

Industrial waste can also be re-used and recycled. Waste materials can be burnt and the heat used to keep buildings warm. New technologies are being developed to reduce and control pollution. The American company, Dow Chemical, has a 'Waste Reduction Always Pays' policy and has saved millions of dollars by recycling materials that were previously wasted. At one of its British factories, Dow has reduced waste sent to landfill sites by 50 per cent. In the USA, waste recycling and pollution control have become major industries employing thousands of people. It shows that improving the environment can be good business.

What you can do
Use things again whenever possible and if something can't be re-used see if it can be recycled. Use bottle and metal can banks. Don't buy products that have an unnecessary amount of packaging that is simply thrown away.

CITY LIFE — 1

Urban Explosion

The world population is increasing dramatically. In 1800 it was one billion people, 100 years later it was 1.5 billion but only 50 years after that in 1950 it was 2.5 billion. It has more than doubled since then and today stands at over 5 billion. Population is growing fastest in the developing world, especially in Africa and Asia.

Cities in the poorer countries are becoming larger as populations grow and as people leave the countryside to look for work and shelter elsewhere. People migrate to cities because they are attracted by the hope of an easier life or because there is no food or work in the countryside. Sometimes the political situation forces them to move.

In 1950, only one African city, Cairo, had a population of over 1 million. It is estimated that by 2000, there will be 60 cities in Africa with over a million people. World-wide, over half the planet's population will live in cities by the end of this century. Cities cannot cope with all these people. They cannot provide the jobs, shelter, heating, food and water needed — many people are homeless, others live on the streets or in terrible conditions in shanty towns. In Ankara, Turkey, shanty-town dwellers or squatters make up 50 per cent of the city's population.

Poverty is also the enemy of the environment. In their struggle for their next meal, poor people are unable to think about taking care of their surroundings, protecting animals or cleaning up rivers.

Living in a shanty town

Shanty towns usually grow up on the outskirts of cities. The shelters are often made from old packing cases, plastic sheeting, wood and even cardboard. There are rarely any basic services such as clean water, lavatories, food or fuel, and these poor conditions can lead to pollution of the environment, diseases and crime.

A shanty town perched on a hillside above Rio de Janeiro in Brazil, not far from the tall skyscrapers and wealthy suburbs of the city.

Key

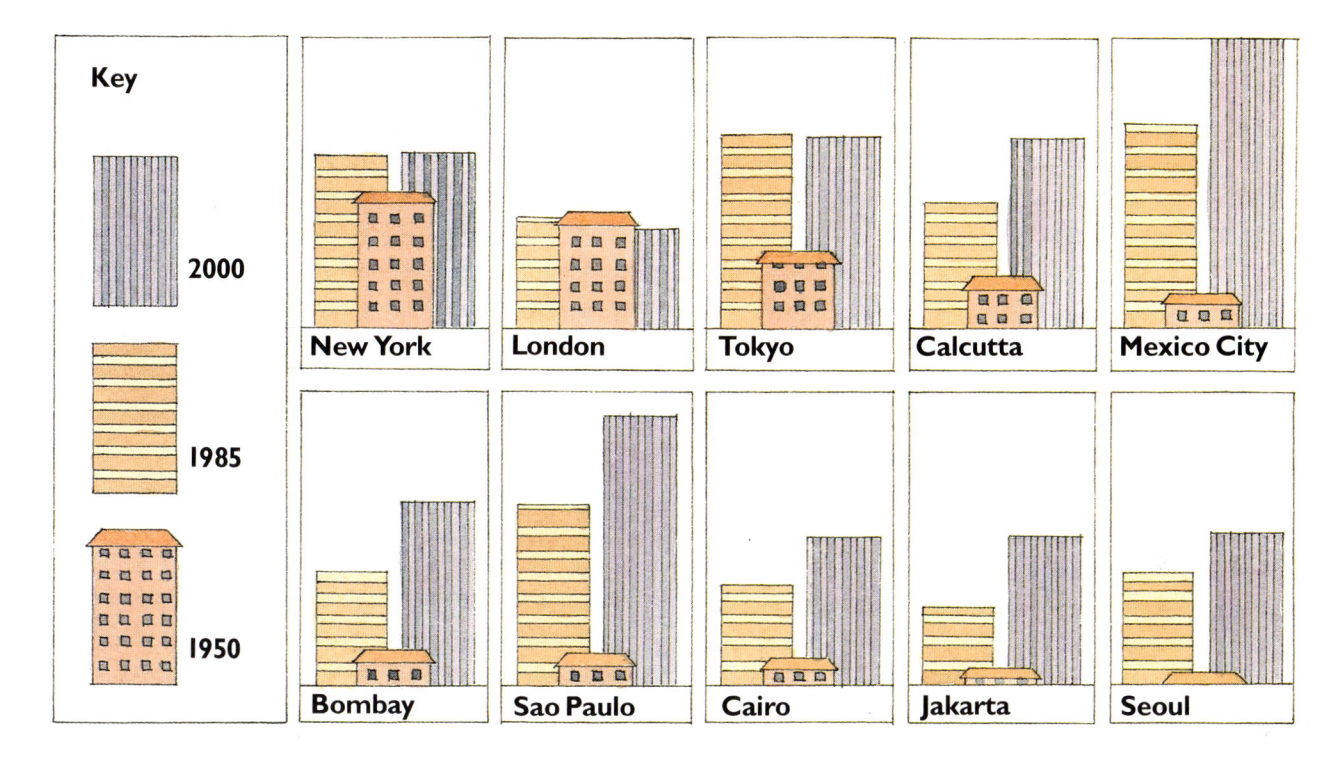

- 2000
- 1985
- 1950

New York | London | Tokyo | Calcutta | Mexico City

Bombay | Sao Paulo | Cairo | Jakarta | Seoul

While most cities in the developed world are getting smaller or growing slowly, many of those in Asia, Africa and South America are expanding at a very fast rate.

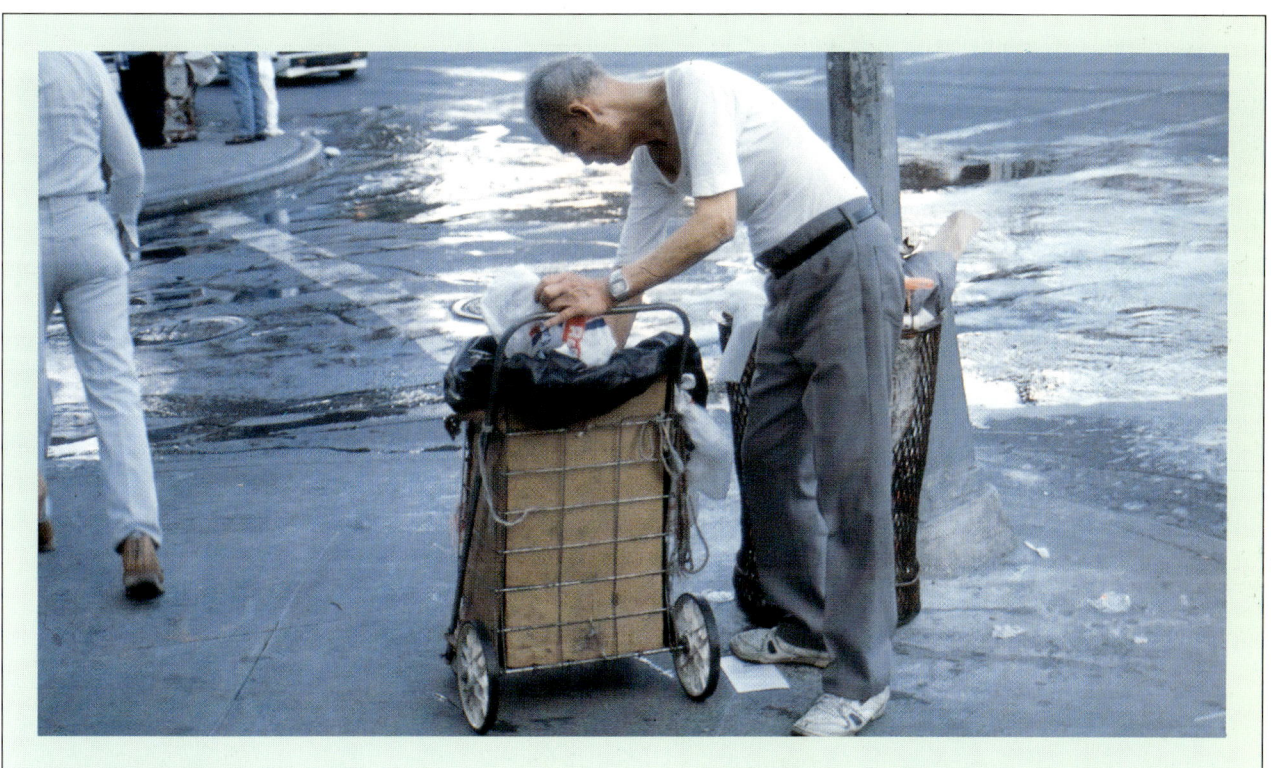

Cities in the North

In the developed world, cities have been urbanized for much longer than in the developing countries. They face a different problem. People are much wealthier and they are leaving cities to live in the suburbs or countryside. The poorer people are left behind and the lack of wealth in the city means that services decline. The cities often become centres for the unemployed, homeless and disadvantaged minorities. This is called inner city decay: it can lead to a rise in crime and violence.

Above This homeless man in New York, USA, carries all his possessions around with him.

CITY LIFE — 2

A Better Life?

How can the quality of life be improved for the millions of poor people in developing world cities? Voluntary organizations such as Oxfam and Save the Children Fund, individuals such as Mother Teresa of Calcutta, and international agencies such as the United Nations Organization, are working to improve conditions. They work with the people and fund projects to provide clean water, roads and energy schemes.

Cities need to be organized and managed, and the best way to do this is by involving the people who live there. By setting up self-help schemes and local community groups, the city-dwellers can organize themselves. But before they can do this, they need to know that they will not be evicted. Only when people are secure will they feel it is worthwhile to improve their home. Low-cost housing, suitable technology, employment opportunities and loans of money are all ways which can help people to improve their lives.

Mother Teresa is one of the many people and organizations working to improve the lives of poor city dwellers in developing countries.

Inner-city regeneration

In the developed world, new life is being brought into cities to halt the inner-city decay. Cities such as Glasgow in Scotland and San Francisco, USA, have been transformed by programmes to restore historic buildings, improve transport and build new homes. Art, sport and recreation events have added to people's enjoyment of city life. Community spirit is the feeling that people belong to an area and any action they take is worthwhile. This spirit has been awakened by the setting up of neighbourhood groups, maybe to paint a mural on a blank wall or to run a city farm. There has also been a movement to make cities greener by planting more trees and providing more open spaces and play areas.

Below Here are some of the ways in which inner-city areas can be improved.

- city farm and park on derelict land
- community centre
- new houses
- old houses modernized
- unused buildings converted to small workshops
- local public transport
- community art
- traffic control

Land-sharing

In Bangkok, Thailand, there are over a million people living in slums and shanty towns. In one area, Manangkasila, a shanty town grew up on public land but in 1978 the government sold the land to a company that wished to develop it commercially. The squatters were given one year to move and were offered compensation. But the squatters protested and even organized demonstrations outside the Prime Minister's house. Eventually, the government, the company and the squatter's community leaders met to discuss the problem and a land-sharing agreement was signed. The community leaders helped to plan new houses on the site and they arranged funds so people could buy these homes.

In some other cities, including Hong Kong, the city authorities provide a site with fresh water, proper sanitation and electricity, and the homeless people then have to build their own houses from whatever materials they can afford. Although they do not provide the luxuries that people in rich countries expect, these sites are much healthier and safer than shanty towns.

CHANGING DIRECTION — 1

The Price of Progress

Many people believe that the time has come to stop and think about the effect we are having on the world. Should we continue to use resources such as oil and trees as if they were in unlimited supply? Oil, for example, will probably run out during the lifetime of people who are being born in the early 1990s, and some metals, such as lead, are unlikely to last for another 50 years. Even resources that nature can replenish, like forests, soil and fish, are being used up faster then they are replaced.

How long can we continue to foul the earth with the wastes that we produce in industry, agriculture and our homes? Dealing with waste costs money and there is a temptation to think that it is cheaper and easier to leave nature to dispose of it instead. The damage to the ozone layer, the warming of the earth caused by the increase in greenhouse gases, and the poisoning of wildlife in rivers and the sea show that the natural processes are being overwhelmed.

While the developed world is getting richer, consuming more and producing more waste, many people in the poorer countries do not even have enough to eat, let alone decent housing, clean water supplies, clothing, health facilities and all the other things that people in the developed world take for granted.

A question of priorities

Today, more food and more goods are being produced than ever before, using more energy and more raw materials. This is also creating more waste. In some cases, the desire of companies and countries to grow richer has been regarded as more important than taking care of the environment and its people. There have been several major catastrophes as a result of the demand for profit at almost any price.

We cannot carry on like this. In future we will have to make valuable resources go further by re-using and recycling them wherever possible. Fuels such as oil and coal cannot be re-used — once burnt they are gone forever — and so we must develop ways of using less of them. And we should not allow the manufacturers of the goods we use to put money before the health of the planet.

Copsa Mica in Romania is thought to be the most polluted town in Europe. It will take many years and a lot of money to clean up such polluted areas.

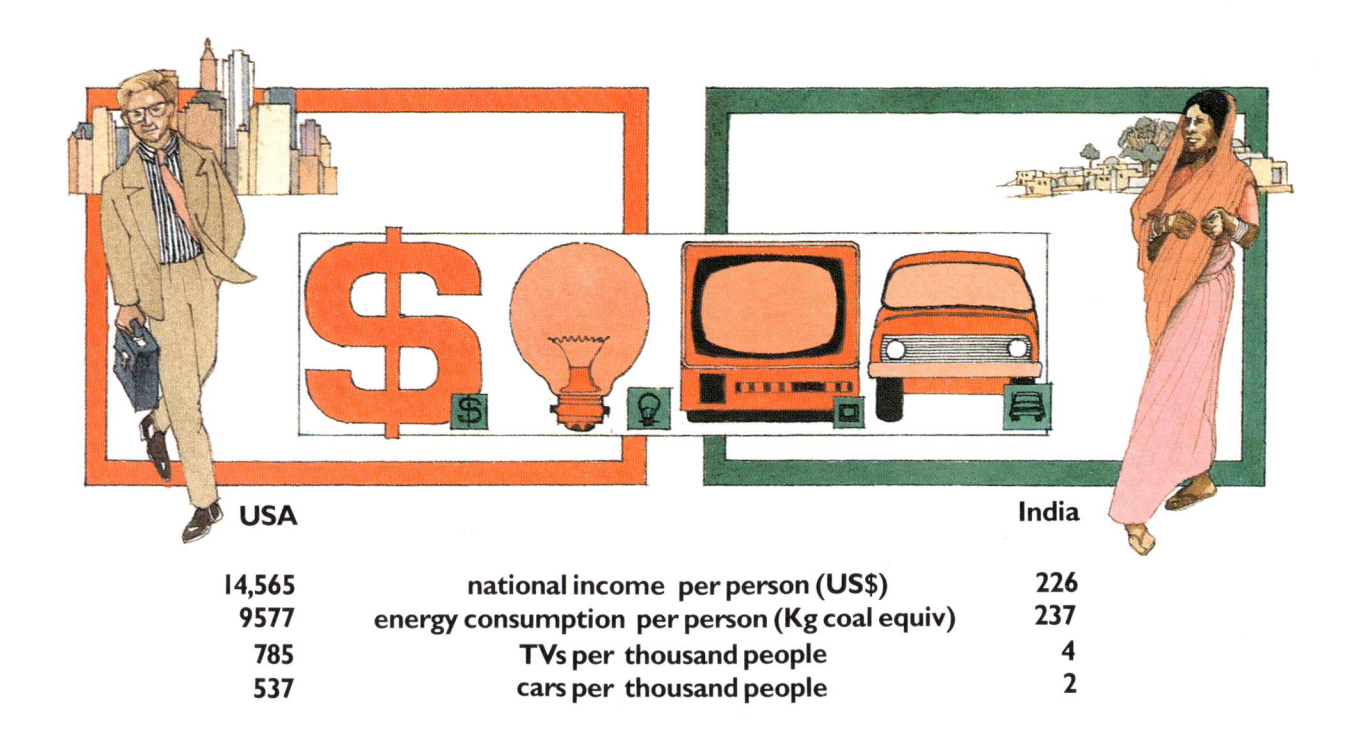

USA		India
14,565	national income per person (US$)	226
9577	energy consumption per person (Kg coal equiv)	237
785	TVs per thousand people	4
537	cars per thousand people	2

Most people in developing countries earn less money, own fewer possessions, use less resources, and have poorer health facilities than those in the developed world.

Bhopal — industry's human cost

Modern industry produces goods that people need and provides jobs. But sometimes the cost can be very high. In 1984 there was an explosion at the Union Carbide chemicals factory in Bhopal, India. A cloud of poisonous gas spread over the surrounding area where many people lived. Almost immediately, 2,500 people died, and more than half a million others are likely to suffer for the rest of their lives as a result of breathing in the gas. It was discovered that this disaster occurred because the factory was not operated safely and its equipment was not properly maintained.

Above Victims of the Bhopal tragedy.

CHANGING DIRECTION — 2

Politics and the Green Movement

The idea that the environment should be protected is not new. Centuries ago, American Indians, Australian Aborigines and many other groups of people developed ways of life that enabled them to live in the environment without damaging it.

Today, especially among the rich nations, there is a growing number of people who aim to introduce new ways of living that will protect the environment. This is called the Green Movement. More people know about the environmental crisis because of campaigns and education. Now more people want to do something to solve the problems. Most countries in Western Europe have green political parties that people can join. There is also a green movement in the USSR, the USA, Canada, New Zealand and Australia. Candidates have been elected into national governments in Germany and Tasmania, where they can help change policies.

Some of the environmental problems are so large that they will only be solved if countries cooperate with each other. The United Nations Environment Programme brings governments together to solve problems. Agreements have already been reached on the ozone layer, acid rain and pollution of the sea.

Arms and the environment

Looking after the earth more carefully will cost a lot of money, but it will cost far less than the amount that is spent on building up the world's armies and their stockpiles of weapons. About US$800 billion is spent each year on military projects — more than the total earned by the poorest half of the world's population. If world peace and stability could be achieved, this money could be used for protecting the earth.

A Soviet cameraman films the dismantling of American Pershing II missiles in Germany. Friendly relations between the world's major military powers should bring what is called a 'peace dividend' — money can be spent on the environment instead of on weapons.

Successful green action

In Tasmania, Australia, the green movement managed to stop the construction of a dam that would have flooded vast areas of natural forest and caves containing prehistoric paintings. The area has now been made into a World Heritage Site and it cannot be developed.

In the USA, members of a green organization called Earth First take direct action to protect the environment. In California they prevented some of the world's oldest and tallest trees from being cut down by sitting 30 metres up in the branches.

These are only two examples of the many successes that have been achieved. Nonetheless, there is still much to be done, and our fragile earth can only be saved if we all care enough to try.

Below People in Budapest, Hungary, protesting against environmental damage.

Events seem to be moving in the right direction. In recent years there have been talks between the USSR and the USA that have resulted in both superpowers reducing their nuclear and conventional weapons. In 1989 and 1990 dramatic changes took place in many countries in Eastern Europe. Partly as a result of encouragement from President Gorbachev of the USSR, millions of people were able to free themselves from the Communist rule under which they lived for many years, and elect their own democratic governments.

Although some parts of the world appear to be becoming safe, the Gulf Crisis that began in August 1990 — when Iraq invaded neighbouring Kuwait and several Western countries responded by sending arms and troops to the area — showed that world peace will not be easy to achieve. However, if our planet is to have a future the world's political leaders must continue to talk and learn to solve their differences peacefully.

What you can do

There are lots of organizations that provide information about the ways in which they are trying to ensure the survival of the planet. Many of them have special sections for young people — join one that interests you. Above all, don't forget that the future depends on all of us.

Glossary

Acid rain Rain is normally slightly acid. Gases produced by the burning of fossil fuels can combine in the air to produce strongly acid pollution that can fall as a dry dust or as acid rain, mist or snow.

Atmosphere The layer of gases, water vapour and dust that surrounds the earth. The gases are nitrogen (78%), oxygen (21%), argon (1%), and very small amounts of carbon dioxide, neon, ozone, hydrogen and krypton. The amount of water vapour varies.

Cancer A type of disease caused by the growth of abnormal cells in the body of a human or other animal.

Catalytic converter A device fitted to vehicle exhausts to reduce the amount of pollution they emit.

Chlorofluorocarbons (CFCs) A group of chemicals that cause damage to the ozone layer above the earth.

Commercial Done to make a profit.

Contaminate To pollute or make impure.

Culture A society's traditions, including its language, religion, art, music and legends.

Developed countries The richer, industrialized countries of the world, including the USA, Australia, Japan and European countries.

Developing countries The poorer countries of the world such as some African, Asian and South American countries.

Dioxins A group of chemicals that include some of the most poisonous chemicals known.

Environment The surroundings of a plant or animal, including the air, soil and water.

European Community (EC) A union of European countries formed in 1957. There are now twelve members: Belgium, France, Italy, Luxembourg, the Netherlands, Germany, Denmark, the Republic of Ireland, Britain, Spain, Portugal and Greece.

Food chain A chain of living things that depend on each other for food. For example, grass is eaten by sheep which are eaten by humans.

Fossil fuels Fuels such as oil, coal and natural gas that were produced by the decaying of plants that lived millions of years ago.

Global warming The increase in the earth's temperature caused by the build-up of greenhouse gases in the atmosphere.

Greenhouse gases The gases in the atmosphere which slow down the rate at which heat from the earth escapes into space.

Hydroelectricity Energy that is generated from the movement of water.

Landfills Dump sites where waste is thrown and the ground filled in.

Migration The regular or permanent movement of people from one place to another.

Nuclear power station A power station in which electricity is generated from the decay of radioactive 'fuel', such as uranium.

Ozone layer A thin layer of ozone gas in the upper atmosphere which filters out the sun's harmful ultraviolet rays.

PCBs (Polychlorinated biphenyls) A group of highly poisonous chemicals.

Pesticides Chemicals used to kill plant or animal pests.

Pollution The release of harmful materials into the air, water or land that may upset the balance of the environment.

Prehistoric From a time before writing was first invented.

Radioactive A word to describe a material that gives out dangerous rays, or radiation, when it breaks down or decays.

Rainforest An area of dense, tropical forest.

Recycling The processing of waste materials so that they can be used again.

Renewable energy Sources of energy that do not use up resources which cannot be replaced.

Resource Anything which is useful to living plants and animals (including humans).

Sanitation A system aimed at protecting people's health against dirt and infection.

Sewage The waste from homes and industry that is flushed down the sink, drain or toilet.

Stratosphere The layer of the atmosphere from about 16km to 50km above the earth.

Toxic Harmful or poisonous.

Tropical A word describing the hot, wet climate in parts of the world between the tropics, on either side of the equator.

Turbine A machine in which the energy of moving water, air or steam causes a blade to spin, usually to generate electricity.

Ultraviolet rays Invisible light from the sun which can damage plants and animals if they are exposed to too much of it.

United Nations Organization The international organization that brings together all the countries of the world to discuss world problems.

Uranium A radioactive substance used as a source of nuclear energy.

Urbanization The making of rural areas into towns and cities.

Further Information

If you want to find out more about the ways in which the earth is being damaged and the organizations that are trying to prevent it, you might like to contact some of the groups at the addresses listed here and read some of the books below.

Useful addresses

Australia:
  Australian Conservation Foundation
  GPO Box 1875, Canberra ACT 2601

  Friends of the Earth
  366 Smith Street, Collingwood VIC 3066

  Greenpeace
  785 George Street, Sydney NSW 2000

Britain:
  Acid Rain Information Centre
  Department of Environmental and
  Geographic Studies
  Manchester Polytechnic, John Dalton
  Extension
  Chester Street, Manchester M1 5GD

  Friends of the Earth
  26-28 Underwood Street, London N1 7JQ

  Greenpeace
  30-31 Islington Green, London N1 8XE

  National Society for Clean Air
  136 North Street, Brighton BN1 1RG

  NIREX Information Centre
  Curie Avenue, Harwell, Didcot
  Oxon OX11 0RH

  Survival International
  310 Edgware Road, London W2 1DY

  WATCH
  The Green, Witham Park, Lincoln LN5 7JR

Canada:
  Greenpeace
  427 Bloor Street West, Toronto
  Ontario M5S 1X7

  Pollution Probe
  12 Madison Avenue, Toronto
  Ontario M5R 2S1

International:
  Greenpeace International
  Keizersgracht 176
  1016 DW Amsterdam, The Netherlands

  United Nations Environment Programme
  PO Box 30552, Nairobi, Kenya

New Zealand:
  Environment and Conservation
  Organizations of New Zealand Inc (ECO)
  PO Box 11057, Wellington

  Friends of the Earth
  Nagal House, Courthouse Lane
  PO Box 39/065, Auckland West

USA:
  Friends of the Earth
  530 7th Street SE, Washington DC 20003
  and
  1045 Sansome Street, San Francisco
  CA 94111

  Greenpeace
  1436 U Street NW, Washington DC 20009

  National Campaign Against Toxic Hazards
  2000 P Street NW, Washington DC 20009

Books to read

Acid Rain by J. Baines (Wayland, 1989)
Atlas of Environmental Issues by N. Middleton (Oxford University Press, 1988)
The Climate Crisis — Greenhouse Effect and Ozone Layer by J. Beckdale (Franklin Watts, 1989)
Conserving the Atmosphere by J. Baines (Wayland, 1989)
The Dying Sea by M. Bright (Franklin Watts, 1988)
Ecology by R. Spurgeon (Usborne, 1988)
The Environment by A. Markham (Wayland, 1988)
The Gaia Atlas of Planet Management edited by N. Myers (Pan, 1985)
Pollution by M. Gittins (National Society for Clean Air, 1983)
Toxic Waste and Recycling by N. Hawkes (Franklin Watts, 1988)
Waste and Recycling by B. James (Wayland, 1989)

Index

Acid rain 14-17, 40
Agricultural pollution 30, 38
Aluminium 14
Alzheimer's disease 14
American Indians 26-7, 40
Antarctica 6, 10, 12
Arctic 10
Australia 10, 26, 28, 29, 40, 41
Australian Aborigines 26, 28, 29, 40
Austria 16

Bangladesh 6
Bhopal 39
Bottle banks 32, 33
Brazil 11, 16, 26, 34
Britain 10, 14, 17, 18, 31, 33
Bushmen of the Kalahari 26

Canada 14, 33, 40
Cancer 10, 30
Carbon cycle 9
Cars 14, 16, 17
Catalytic converter 16
CFCs (chlorofluorocarbons) 6, 7, 9, 10, 11, 12, 13
Chernobyl 18, 19
Cities 34-7
Climatic change 6, 7

Drought 6
Dry storage 25

Earth First 41
Energy efficiency 9
Energy saving 9, 20-21
European Community (EC) 16

Forests 7, 9, 14, 38
Fossil fuels 6, 7, 9, 14, 18
Friends of the Earth 13, 24

Gaia 8
Geothermal power 19, 21
Germany 16, 40
Global warming 6-9, 38
Gorbachev, Mikhail 41
Greece 15
Greenhouse effect 6-9, 14
Greenhouse gases 6, 7, 8, 38
Green Movement 40
Greenpeace 13, 24, 33

Guatemala 9

Half-life 22
Homelessness 34, 35, 37
Hong Kong 37
Hoover Dam 21
Hungary 41
Hydroelectric power 19, 20, 21

Iceland 12, 21
Incinerator ships 30
Industrial pollution 14, 38
Inner-city decay 35
Inuit 28
Iraq 41

Japan 5

Karin B 31
Kuwait 41

Lakes 14
Landfill sites 30, 33
Land-sharing agreements 37-8
Lead-free petrol 14, 16
Lovelock, James 8

Montreal Protocol 12
Mother Teresa 36

New Zealand 40
Nigeria 31
NIREX 24, 25
Norway 16, 20
Nuclear energy 18-21, 22
Nuclear waste 19, 22-5
    dumping 23, 24, 25
    reprocessing 22
    storage 23, 25

Oxfam 36
Ozone layer 10-13, 14, 38, 40

PCBs 30, 31, 33
Peace dividend 40
Pesticides 30, 31
Plutonium 22
Population 34
Power stations 7, 9, 14, 19, 20, 21, 23, 25
Public transport 17, 21

Radioactive decay 22, 23
Recycling 8, 32, 33
Romania 38

Save the Children Fund 36
Self-help schemes 36, 37
Sellafield 22
Senegal 8
Sewage 30, 38
Shanty towns 34, 37
Solar power 8, 19, 25
Surival International 29
Sweden 16
Switzerland 16

Thailand 37
Tidal power 19, 25
Toxic waste 30-33
Tribal peoples 26-29
Turkey 34

Ultraviolet radiation 10, 14
United Nations Environment Programme 8, 40
United Nations Organization 36
Uranium 18, 22
USA 6, 12, 15, 16, 21, 30, 33, 35, 37, 40, 41
USSR 19, 40, 41

Vehicle exhaust gases 6, 7, 14, 16
Venezuela 26

Wave power 19, 25
Weapons expenditure 40
Wind power 19, 20, 25
World Conservation Union 8

Yanomami Indians 26